UAE Vibrant City, Beaches, Mountains, Deserts and Adventure: The Ultimate Abu Dhabi Experience and must-see sights

Abu Dhabi
Travel Guide 2023

ROLAND RICHARD

Table of Contents

Etihad Towers, Abu Dhabi

Chapter 1

Introduction

Overview of Abu Dhabi

Welcome to Abu Dhabi, the fascinating crown jewel of the United Arab Emirates (UAE) and a place where heritage and modernity coexist in perfect harmony.

Abu Dhabi, whose name translates to "Father of the Gazelle," has a long history that extends back to its days as a fishing and pearl-diving community.

Travellers from all over the world are in for a captivating experience in Abu Dhabi, which is tucked away on the shores of the Arabian

Gulf. This booming town, known for its beautiful architecture, cultural diversity, and luxury amenities, promises an enchanted journey.

It now stands as a testament to ingenuity and progress, extending friendly Arabian hospitality to all who enter.

Abu Dhabi's Interesting History

Discover the fascinating past that helped to create the vibrant metropolis that is Abu Dhabi today. Abu Dhabi's history is a tapestry of cultural influences and strategic growth, from its early days as a Bedouin community to its rise as the capital of the UAE.

Learn about the important role that the Al Nahyan family played in influencing the course of the city, as they have been the monarchy since the 18th century.

Discover the tales of the Bedouin tribes, traders, and pearl divers who contributed to the region's rich history.

Learn about Abu Dhabi's rise to prominence and how it went from having a pearl economy to an oil-rich one. Explore the historical sites and archaeological digs that reveal traces of the city's colourful past.

Abu Dhabi in 2023: New and Exciting Developments

As a result of the city's commitment to innovation and sustainable development, there is always something new to discover.

Discover the newest additions to Abu Dhabi's skyline, including remarkable structures that push the limits of engineering and architecture. Modern museums, cutting-edge entertainment centres, and top-notch retail areas will enthral you.

Events ranging from international sporting competitions to cultural festivals that highlight the city's rich history will be held in Abu Dhabi in 2023.

Take part in the festivities that showcase Emirati customs and beliefs.

Abu Dhabi's natural beauties will take the stage in 2023, with a focus on eco-friendly projects. Observe the city's dedication to protecting its breathtaking desert vistas, beautiful oasis, and varied fauna.

Be prepared to be astounded as Abu Dhabi redefines luxury by providing visitors with privileged experiences and unmatched hospitality.

Abu Dhabi in 2023 is a location that promises to surpass your expectations and leave you with memories to enjoy for a lifetime, whether you're a history enthusiast, an admirer of architecture, or a seeker of fresh experiences.

Accept the attraction of this vibrant city, where tradition and modernity coexist together. Welcome to Abu Dhabi, where you are in for the experience of a lifetime.

Chapter 2

Planning Your Trip

The Best Time to Visit Abu Dhabi in 2023:

Visiting Abu Dhabi at the ideal time will greatly improve your trip. The city will provide a wide variety of activities and events in 2023. To properly plan your journey, take into account the seasons:

- **Winter (November to March)**: Abu Dhabi is most frequently visited during the winter months because of the excellent weather and temperatures that range from 20°C to 30°C (68°F to 86°F).

Outdoor activities, cultural exploration, and visiting numerous festivals and events are all ideal during this period.

- **Spring (April to May)**: With an average temperature of roughly 25°C (77°F), springtime is known for its pleasant weather.

Exploring outdoor sites, going on desert excursions, and taking in flowering vistas are all fantastic things to do now.

- **Summer (June to September)**: The summer season is quite hot, with average highs exceeding 40°C (104°F).

Although hotel rates may be lower at this time, the intense heat makes outdoor activities difficult. Malls and indoor attractions, however, offer relief from the heat.

- **Autumn (October)**: Autumn is a transitional season in Abu Dhabi, with temperatures beginning to drop.

It's a great time for vacationers on a tight budget because hotel rates are lower than they are during the busiest winter months.

The ideal time to go ultimately depends on your tastes and heat tolerance. Plan your vacation for the winter or spring when the weather is nice for a relaxing experience.

Visa Requirements and Travel Papers

It's crucial to make sure you have the required visas and travel papers before beginning your trip to Abu Dhabi in 2023.

Depending on your nationality, the criteria may change, therefore it's critical to review the most recent regulations well in advance. Here are some important things to think about:

- **Passport**: Make sure your passport is valid for at least six more months than the day you intend to depart from Abu Dhabi.

- **Visa**: For short visits, many nationalities qualify for a visa-on-arrival or visa exemption. However, it's imperative to apply for the necessary visa in advance for longer visits.

- **Tourist Visa**: You can often apply for a tourist visa through one of the UAE's official channels if you're planning a vacation to Abu Dhabi.

- **Business Visa**: Make sure to apply for the proper business visa if you intend to travel to Abu Dhabi for business.

Choosing the Best Accommodation for Your Stay

Abu Dhabi provides a variety of lodging choices to fit any traveller's needs and price range. Finding the ideal lodging is crucial for a good visit, whether you are looking for luxury resorts, boutique hotels, or affordable accommodations. Think about the following elements:

- **Location**: Pick a place that fits with your travel schedule. In contrast to beachside properties, which offer breathtaking vistas and waterfront activities, downtown Abu Dhabi provides quick access to the city's top attractions and commercial areas.

- **Wifi**: Search for hotels with services like Wi-Fi, swimming pools, fitness centres, spa facilities, and on-site dining that meet your needs.
- **Ratings and reviews**: To learn more about the hotel's level of service, cleanliness, and overall experience, read reviews written by past visitors.
- **Budget**: Abu Dhabi has lodgings for all price points, so set yours in advance and look for places to stay that go well with your financial strategy.

Essentials to Bring for a Memorable Trip

You can guarantee a smooth and comfortable journey to Abu Dhabi by packing thoughtfully. Include the following necessities on your packing list:

- **Pack breathable, lightweight clothing** appropriate for the season of your trip. Bring light-coloured, loose-fitting clothing in the summer to stay comfortable, and think about layering in the winter for the chilly evenings.

- **Sun protection**: The sun in Abu Dhabi may be very strong, so be sure to bring sunscreen, sunglasses, a wide-brimmed hat, and a scarf or shawl to shield yourself.

- **Travel Documents**: Make sure you have your passport, visa, travel insurance, and tickets with you at all times.
- **Medication**: Bring any prescription drugs you might require, as well as a basic first-aid kit for any minor aches or pains.
- **Adaptor and chargers**: Because Abu Dhabi uses a Type G plug for electrical outlets, you should pack the proper adaptor and chargers for your electronic equipment.
- **Reusable Water Bottle**: It's important to stay hydrated, especially in the

summer. Bring a reusable water bottle with you so you may fill it up as needed.

- **Comfortable Shoes**: Bring a pair of sandals for the beach or poolside as well as comfortable walking shoes for seeing local sights.

By taking into account these factors and planning appropriately, you'll create the ideal conditions for an outstanding trip to Abu Dhabi in 2023.

Have fun on your trip, and may it be full of excitement, learning, and priceless memories.

Chapter 3

Top Attractions in Abu Dhabi

Sheikh Zayed Grand Mosque: A Work of Islamic Art

Location: Abu Dhabi, United Arab Emirates, Sheikh Rashid Bin Saeed Street

Prepare to be awestruck by the Sheikh Zayed Grand Mosque's magnificence, an architectural marvel that serves as a symbol of Abu Dhabi's cultural legacy.

This magnificent mosque is one of the world's largest, with beautiful marble work, brilliant chandeliers, and delicate floral decorations.

Visitors are invited to observe the 82 white marble domes and the mesmerising reflection pools that add to the ethereal splendour of the structure.

The mosque's quiet ambience and peaceful surroundings make it a must-see site for visitors interested in learning about the city's Islamic past.

The Louvre Abu Dhabi: Where Art and Culture Meet

Location: Abu Dhabi, United Arab Emirates, Saadiyat Cultural District

The Louvre Abu Dhabi, a cultural icon that celebrates the universal spirit of creativity, promises an encounter with art and culture.

This one-of-a-kind museum displays a remarkable collection of art spanning centuries and countries, allowing visitors to see how human civilizations are interrelated.

Admire artwork from both the Eastern and Western traditions, including masterpieces by renowned painters and compelling shows that cross the cultural divide.

The contemporary design of the Louvre Abu Dhabi, built on a floating island, provides an unmatched experience that speaks to the heart of any art enthusiast.

Thrills, Adventure, and Entertainment on Yas Island

Yas Island is a haven for thrill seekers and adventurers alike. It has a plethora of world-class attractions, making it a must-see destination for both families and single travellers.

Feel the rush of adrenaline at Ferrari World Abu Dhabi, an indoor entertainment park devoted to the legendary Italian automobile company, Ferrari.

Experience record-breaking roller coasters and exhilarating thrills that will leave you speechless. Next, visit Yas Waterworld, a water park that promises aquatic thrills for all ages, from exhilarating water slides to a relaxing lazy river.

Yas Marina Circuit hosts the Formula 1 Abu Dhabi Grand Prix, a stunning annual event for motorsport lovers.

Golfers will enjoy the Yas Links Golf Club, which provides a picturesque and challenging golfing experience.

Yas Island also has gorgeous beaches, elegant hotels, and a vibrant nightlife scene, making it a dynamic entertainment and leisure destination.

Discovering the Cultural Oasis of Saadiyat Island

Location: *Saadiyat Island is located in Abu Dhabi, United Arab Emirates.*

Saadiyat Island, a hub of art, culture, and natural beauty, is a cultural paradise. The island is home to many world-class attractions, including the renowned Saadiyat Cultural District, which houses the Louvre Abu Dhabi and other museums. Art lovers will enjoy the regular art exhibitions, workshops, and cultural events held here.

The Zayed National Museum and the Guggenheim Abu Dhabi (under construction) are both located on Saadiyat

Island, adding a complement to the region's cultural landscape.

Saadiyat Beach is perfect for nature lovers, with its beautiful shoreline and clear blue waves, making it an ideal site for relaxation and beach sports.

Relaxation by the Azure Waters at Corniche Beach

Location: Corniche Road in Abu Dhabi, United Arab Emirates

Relax at Corniche Beach, a beautiful length of shoreline that runs for many kilometres along the city's waterfront.

Corniche Beach, with its silky, golden sands and crystal-clear seas, is a sanctuary for beachgoers and watersports aficionados.

The seashore features well-kept walkways, lush gardens, and covered spaces that are ideal for picnics and strolls.

Enjoy a variety of water sports, beach volleyball, or simply relax in the sun and admire Abu Dhabi's magnificent skyline.

Corniche Beach is a popular destination for both locals and tourists looking for peace and pleasure in the middle of the city.

Exploring the Presidential Palace in Qasr Al Watan

Location: *Abu Dhabi, United Arab Emirates, Al Ras Al Akhdar*

The Presidential Palace, Qasr Al Watan, is located in the centre of Abu Dhabi's governance and history.

This regal landmark welcomes visitors, providing a rare peek into the UAE's political and cultural history.

Admire the palace's unique Arabian decor, which includes dazzling chandeliers, hand-woven rugs, and sumptuous accents.

Visitors can wander among the numerous chambers, halls, and displays that highlight the country's governance traditions as well as contributions to art, science, and knowledge.

These top Abu Dhabi attractions offer a unique and enriching travel experience, allowing tourists to immerse themselves in the city's past, culture, and modern delights.

Abu Dhabi provides something for every traveller's heart, from architectural marvels to exhilarating excursions and tranquil beaches.

Chapter 4

Cultural Experiences and Festivals

Hospitality and Traditions of Emirati Culture

Learn about Emirati customs and etiquette to immerse yourself in the rich Emirati culture. Emiratis are noted for their friendliness and adherence to tradition. As a guest, you must be aware of the following cultural norms:

- **Greetings**: Because Emiratis cherish greetings, it is traditional to greet someone with a polite "As-salam Alaykum" (peace be upon you). "Wa

Alaykum as-salam" (peace be upon you) is the appropriate response.

- While Abu Dhabi is modern and cosmopolitan, **modest attire is preferred**, especially in public places and religious sites.

  Wearing clothes that cover the shoulders and knees is considered courteous.

- **Public shows of Affection**: Public shows of affection are not culturally suitable. Avoid displaying rage or dissatisfaction in public, as Emiratis admire calmness.

- **Ramadan Etiquette**: If you visit during Ramadan (the Islamic holy month), keep in mind that it is a fasting period from sunrise to sunset.

As a courtesy, avoid eating, drinking, or smoking in public during daylight hours.

Emirati Cuisine: Experiment with Your Taste Buds

Taste the flavours of Emirati cuisine, which is a delectable combination of Arabian, Persian, Indian, and African influences. Enjoy classic dishes that highlight the region's distinct culinary heritage:

- **Machbous**: A fragrant rice dish flavoured with aromatic spices and cooked with meat (usually lamb or chicken).

- **Harees**: A savoury porridge comprised of pounded wheat and beef that has been slow-cooked to perfection.
- **Luqaimat**:Sweet,deep-fried dumplings coated with date syrup or honey, a popular festival treat.
- **Shawarma**: Marinated meat, usually chicken or beef, roasted on a vertical spit and served with various condiments on flatbread.
- **Arabic Coffee**: Enjoy the hospitality of the Emiratis with a cup of authentic

Arabic coffee (Gahwa) served in miniature cups with dates.

Shopping in Abu Dhabi: Traditional Souks and Modern Malls

Abu Dhabi provides an enjoyable shopping experience by combining historic souks with modern shopping malls:

- **Souk Al-Mina**: Visit the traditional marine market, Souk Al-Mina, for fresh seafood, spices, and one-of-a-kind handicrafts.
- **Souk Al Zafarana**: Take in the bright atmosphere of Souk Al Zafarana, which is famed for its colourful textiles, perfumes, and traditional clothes.

- **The Galleria Al Maryah Island**: The Galleria is a high-end mall that houses international designer labels as well as gourmet dining alternatives.
- **Yas Mall**: Located on Yas Island, Yas Mall offers a variety of popular apparel labels, entertainment zones, and culinary options.

Abu Dhabi will be alive with a plethora of festivals and events in 2023, offering unique insights into the city's cultural and social fabric. Among the notable festivals to attend during your visit are:

- **Abu Dhabi Festival**: An annual arts and culture celebration comprising music performances, dance shows, and art exhibitions by local and international artists.

- **UAE National Day**: Held on December 2nd, this happy festival remembers the founding of the UAE with parades, fireworks, and a variety of cultural events.

- **Abu Dhabi International Book Fair**: Book lovers will enjoy this literary festival, which features a diverse selection of books, writers, and publishing houses from around the world.

- **Qasr Al Hosn Festival**: This festival, held at the historic Qasr Al Hosn fort, provides a glimpse into Abu Dhabi's legacy with traditional activities, crafts, and performances.

Participating in these festivals and events allows you to interact with the local population, see their cultural manifestations, and build long-lasting memories of your time in Abu Dhabi.

Celebrate the spirit of harmony and variety that defines this interesting location by embracing the city's rich traditions.

Chapter 5

Outdoor Adventures and Desert Safari

Desert Safari: A Memorable Adventure

Experience an amazing desert safari, a must-do in Abu Dhabi that promises an unforgettable journey across the golden dunes.

Buckle up for a thrilling ride through the vast desert terrain in a 4x4 off-road vehicle. Feel the rush of adrenaline as your expert driver negotiates the undulating dunes, producing an adrenaline-pumping journey.

Prepare for a wonderful evening at a typical Bedouin-style camp as the sun sets over the horizon. Enjoy cultural activities like belly dancing and Tanoura shows while dining under the stars over a sumptuous BBQ meal.

During this incredible desert safari, capture the stunning desert sunset and make unforgettable memories.

Al Ain Oasis Exploration: A Verdant Paradise

Escape to Al Ain's lush oasis, a serene retreat buried in the desert. The Al Ain Oasis is a UNESCO World Heritage site and one of the UAE's oldest continually cultivated landscapes.

Stroll through the shady lanes lined with thousands of date palms, old falaj irrigation systems, and lovely gardens.

Discover the region's agricultural heritage by learning about the ancient farming practices still used by locals.

Al Ain Oasis provides a tranquil refuge from the hustle and bustle of the city, making it a great location for a quiet nature walk and an opportunity to reconnect with nature.

Dhow Cruise: Sail Abu Dhabi's Calm Waters

A dhow sail around the calm waters of the Arabian Gulf allows you to experience the allure of Abu Dhabi's maritime history.

Dhows are historic wooden boats used by Emiratis for generations, and a voyage on one provides a nostalgic peek into the city's past.

Relax onboard as you ride through iconic locations including the Corniche and Abu Dhabi's spectacular skyline.

Choose between day and evening cruises, both of which provide magnificent vistas and photo opportunities.

During this beautiful dhow cruise experience, enjoy a delectable buffet of foreign cuisine and soak in the tranquil ambience.

Wildlife Encounters: Exploring the Biodiversity of Abu Dhabi

Abu Dhabi has various ecosystems that support a diverse range of flora and wildlife. Discover the city's commitment to wildlife conservation and biodiversity through the following experiences:

- **Sir Bani Yas Island**: Sir Bani Yas Island is a natural reserve located off the coast of Abu Dhabi that offers spectacular wildlife encounters.

Take a safari drive or a guided walk to see free-roaming creatures including Arabian oryx, cheetahs and giraffes.

- **Mangrove Kayaking**: Take a kayaking excursion through Abu Dhabi's coastal mangroves.

  Paddle through the tranquil mangrove woodlands, looking for rare bird species, crabs, and other marine life.

- **Houbara Conservation Centre**: Visit the Sheikh Khalifa Houbara Conservation Centre to learn about conservation efforts to protect the endangered Houbara bustard.

Witness the bird's breeding and recuperation process, which helps to conserve this gorgeous species.

Because of Abu Dhabi's dedication to maintaining its natural heritage, these wildlife encounters are both informative and rewarding for nature enthusiasts and wildlife lovers.

Chapter 6

Family-Friendly Abu Dhabi

Are you up for an exciting family experience in Abu Dhabi? There is no need to look any further!

Abu Dhabi is a treasure trove of thrilling events for people of all ages, offering an amazing family trip. Let's get started on the adventure that awaits you:

Yas Waterworld: Fun in the Sun

Yas Waterworld, where exhilarating water activities await, is ready to make a splash! This water park offers it all, from heart-pounding rides to soothing water play zones.

Tot's Playground is ideal for children, while teens and adults can race down the Falcon's Falaj or brave the Liwa Loop.

The thrills never stop as families float down the Al Raha River or ride the gigantic Bandit Bomber roller coaster. Yas Waterworld is the ultimate water playground where the pleasure never stops.

Ferrari World Abu Dhabi: For Thrill-Seekers of All Ages

Buckle up for an action-packed day at Ferrari World Abu Dhabi! This indoor theme park caters to both speed aficionados and families.

Experience the world's fastest roller coaster, Formula Rossa, as it rockets to Formula 1 speeds. Children can enjoy the Junior GT circuit or interact with their favourite Ferrari characters.

Don't miss the Ferrari Past and Present Exhibition, which provides an immersive look at the company's racing history. Ferrari World promises a high-octane journey that will excite your entire family.

Meet Your Favourite Characters at Warner Bros. World Abu Dhabi

At this gigantic indoor theme park, enter the enchanting world of Warner Bros. characters. Six immersive regions bring your favourite superheroes and cartoon characters to life.

In Scooby-Doo: The Museum of Mysteries, join the Mystery Inc. gang and explore Metropolis with Superman. The Cartoon Junction and Bedrock areas provide hours of entertainment for children.

At Warner Bros. World Abu Dhabi, guests can expect live entertainment, exhilarating rides, and interactive experiences.

Family-Friendly Parks and Playgrounds

Khalifa Park is a great combination of amusement rides, stunning gardens, and the opportunity to study at the marine museum.

The huge green spaces and playgrounds of Umm Al Emarat Park encourage children to run and play freely.

Kayak trips through lush mangroves are available at the Mangrove National Park, making for an exciting nature adventure.

Not to mention Heritage Park, where Emirati traditions are brought to life through interactive exhibitions. Each park guarantees treasured family time and outdoor recreation.

Abu Dhabi is the ideal family getaway, with a plethora of fascinating adventures to suit all interests and age groups.

Prepare to be wowed by daring water attractions, high-speed roller coasters, meet-and-greets with legendary characters, and unique outdoor activities.

As you and your family discover the delights of Abu Dhabi, your excitement and joy will be contagious. So pack your luggage, assemble your loved ones, and prepare to embark on an unforgettable family-friendly vacation in the heart of the UAE!

Chapter 7

Nightlife and Entertainment

Nightlife in Abu Dhabi: Clubs, Bars, and Lounges

As the sun goes down, Abu Dhabi's dynamic nightlife comes to life, with clubs, pubs, and lounges to suit every taste.

The city has it all, from stylish rooftop bars with stunning skyline views to frenetic nightclubs with top DJs.

Yas Island is a popular party destination, with world-class clubs and beachside lounges.

The finest hotels in Abu Dhabi also have sophisticated bars and lounges where you can enjoy unique cocktails and live entertainment.

Experience the city's cosmopolitan culture by dancing the night away or relaxing with friends in a fashionable lounge.

Whether you enjoy the lively energy of a nightclub or the refinement of a sophisticated bar, Abu Dhabi's nightlife will leave you speechless.

Cultural Shows and Performances

Through exciting concerts and shows, you can immerse yourself in Abu Dhabi's rich cultural heritage.

Traditional music and dance events are routinely held at the Abu Dhabi Cultural Foundation and the Emirates Palace, providing a glimpse into the city's creative heritage.

Attend a live presentation of the captivating art of Arabic storytelling known as "Hakawati" for a authentic experience.

Enjoy theatre productions that transport you back in time by highlighting the region's history and folklore.

The city comes alive with a broad spectrum of cultural activities during the Abu Dhabi Festival, from classical music concerts to contemporary dance displays.

As you watch these outstanding performances, embrace the spirit of innovation and cultural expression.

Abu Dhabi Events Calendar: What Will Happen in 2023?

In 2023, Abu Dhabi's events schedule will be jam-packed with fascinating events catering to a wide range of interests and tastes. Keep an eye out for the following upcoming events:

- **Abu Dhabi Grand Prix**: Experience the thrill of Formula One racing in the Abu Dhabi Grand Prix, which takes place at the Yas Marina Circuit.

  Join racing fans from all over the world in cheering on their favourite drivers in this thrilling event.

- **Abu Dhabi International Book Fair**: Bookworms will thrill at the Abu Dhabi International Book Fair, a literary celebration involving book launches, author discussions, and an outstanding display of literary works.

- **Abu Dhabi Art**: Abu Dhabi Art, a prominent art fair that shows contemporary and modern art from around the world, will attract art fans. Explore provocative exhibitions and interact with artists, collectors, and curators.

- **Emirates Palace Ramadan Pavilion**: Experience the timeless ritual of Iftar at the Emirates Palace Ramadan Pavilion during the holy month of Ramadan.

In a sumptuous atmosphere, savour an excellent array of Arabian delicacies.

- **Al Dhafra Festival**: The Al Dhafra Festival celebrates Emirati culture by showcasing traditional competitions such as camel beauty contests, falconry, and heritage arts and crafts.

- **New Year's Eve Party**: Say goodbye to the year with a stunning New Year's Eve party.

The famous landmarks of Abu Dhabi light up the night sky with spectacular fireworks, creating a mesmerising show for both residents and visitors.

The events calendar in Abu Dhabi promises an amazing array of activities and festivals catering to a wide range of interests.

You'll find something to delight and excite you throughout your vacation, whether you're a sports fan, an art lover, or a culture seeker.

Keep an eye on the events schedule to avoid missing out on the exciting events in Abu Dhabi in 2023.

Chapter 8

Practical Tips and Safety

Travelling in Abu Dhabi: Transportation Options

Abu Dhabi has a variety of convenient transport choices for moving around the city, including:

- **Taxis**: Taxis are readily available and provide a comfortable and efficient mode of transportation within the city.

  Typically, the initial rate is roughly 3 AED ($0.82), with an extra 1.82 AED ($0.50) every kilometre. Remember that pricing may differ slightly based on the taxi company.

- **Public Buses**: The Abu Dhabi public bus network is substantial, covering the majority of the city. Standard trips start at 2 AED ($0.55) and expedited journeys start at 4 AED ($1.09).

  Exact charge is required, otherwise, a rechargeable Hafilat card can be purchased for quick payment.

- **The Abu Dhabi Metro system** is currently under construction and will open soon.

It will give an additional convenient way of transportation in the city once it is operating.

- **Car Rental**: If you prefer the freedom of driving, Abu Dhabi offers car rental services. The cost of renting a car varies depending on the kind and duration of the rental, however, prices start at about 150 AED ($41) per day.

  If your licence is not in Arabic or English, you must obtain an international driving licence (IDP).

How to Stay Safe and Healthy on Your Trip

Although Abu Dhabi is a secure city for visitors, the following precautions should always be taken:

- **Respect Local Laws and Customs**: Because Abu Dhabi adheres to Islamic laws and traditions, it is critical to respect local customs, dress modestly in public, and avoid public shows of affection.

- **Stay Hydrated**: The UAE has a hot environment, especially during the summer. Drink plenty of water to stay hydrated, which is quite inexpensive at roughly 2 AED ($0.55) for a 500ml bottle.

- **Sun Protection**: Wear sunscreen, sunglasses, and a hat to protect yourself from the sun's rays, which costs roughly 25 AED ($6.81) for a typical 200ml bottle.

Save critical phone numbers on your phone, such as local emergency services (999) and your country's diplomatic contact.

Travellers' Must-Know Arabic Phrases

While English is commonly spoken in Abu Dhabi, knowing a few simple Arabic words will improve your trip experience and demonstrate respect for the local culture:

- Hello: Marhaba (Mar-ha-ba)

- Thank you: Shukran (Shook-ran)

- Please: Min fadlak (Min fad-lak)

- Yes: Na'am (Na-am)

- No: La (La)

- Excuse me: Law samaht (Law sa-maht)

- How much is this?: Kam hatha? (Kam ha-tha?)

- I need help: Ana bahtaj musa'adah (A-na bah-taj mu-sa-adah)

Currency and Payment Options

The UAE Dirham (AED) is the local currency in Abu Dhabi. Here are some money-saving tips:

- **Currency Exchange**: You can exchange your currency for Dirhams in banks, exchange offices, or ATMs located throughout the city. Although exchange rates fluctuate, banks typically offer attractive rates.

- **Credit Cards**: Major enterprises, hotels, restaurants, and shopping malls accept credit cards.

  The most common credit cards are Visa and Mastercard. Remember that some smaller businesses may prefer cash.

- **Tipping** is not common in Abu Dhabi because service charges are frequently included in invoices.

However, a little gratuity for great service is appreciated.

By remembering these helpful hints, you may make the most of your vacation to Abu Dhabi while also ensuring your safety and having a pleasant travel experience.

Spend your money wisely and spend a pleasant and memorable time experiencing the wonders of this enchanting city!

Chapter 9

Day Trips from Abu Dhabi

Dubai: A Glittering Contrast City

The distance between Abu Dhabi and Dubai is approximately 150 kilometres (93 miles).

Travel time: around 1 hour 30 minutes (by car).

A day excursion to Dubai from Abu Dhabi provides an intriguing contrast between two prominent UAE towns.

Dubai is well-known for its technological marvels, futuristic architecture, and luxurious lifestyle. Here are some highlights to look out for on your day trip:

- **The world's tallest building**, the Burj Khalifa, offers stunning views of Dubai from the observation decks on the 124th and 148th levels.

  The ticket cost for the At The Top experience starts at around 149 AED ($40) per person.

- **The Dubai Mall**: Shopaholics will be delighted by a visit to one of the world's largest retail malls.

  The Dubai Mall has about 1,300 retail establishments, an indoor aquarium, an ice rink, and a variety of restaurants.

- **Dubai Marina**: Enjoy the spectacular waterfront views while strolling down the Dubai Marina Walk, which is lined with elegant cafes and restaurants.

- **Dubai Creek**: Take a classic abra ride over Dubai Creek to experience the old-world beauty of Dubai. Abra rides cost about 1-2 AED ($0.27 - $0.54) per person.

- **Souks**: Visit Dubai's classic souks, such as the Gold Souk and Spice Souk, to bargain for gold jewellery, spices, and souvenirs.

The total cost of a day trip to Dubai from Abu Dhabi (without lunches and shopping) is estimated to be around 200-300 AED ($54-$81) per person.

Al Ain: Cultural and Heritage Oasis

The distance between Abu Dhabi and Al Ain is approximately 160 kilometres (99 miles).

Travel time: around 1 hour 30 minutes (by car).

Al Ain, often known as the "Garden City" in the UAE, provides a peaceful respite from the hustle and bustle of city life.

The city is rich in history and culture, and among the must-see sites are:

- **The verdant Al Ain Oasis**, a UNESCO World Heritage site, with its hundreds of date palms and unique falaj irrigation system, is worth a visit. The oasis is normally free to enter.

- **The Al Ain National Museum**: Explore the region's history and archaeology with displays of Bedouin living, ancient artefacts, and local heritage. The cost of admission is approximately 5 AED ($1.36) per person.

- **Al Jahili For**t: Take a look at the picturesque Al Jahili Fort, which houses a museum and holds cultural events and exhibitions. The cost of admission is around 5 AED ($1.36) per person.

- Drive to the summit of **Jebel Hafeet, the UAE's highest peak**, for panoramic views of the city and surrounding desert scenery.

A day trip to Al Ain from Abu Dhabi is estimated to cost around 20-50 AED ($5 - $14) per person.

Sharjah: A Cultural Adventure

The distance between Abu Dhabi and Sharjah is approximately 170 kilometres (106 miles).

Travel time: around 1 hour 30 minutes (by car).

Sharjah is the UAE's cultural centre, famous for its rich heritage, museums, and traditional souks. Here are some highlights of Sharjah's cultural offerings:

- **Sharjah Heritage Area**: Immerse yourself in the city's history by visiting the Sharjah Heritage Museum and exploring traditional Emirati architecture.

- **Sharjah Museum of Islamic Civilization**: This museum houses an extraordinary collection of Islamic art and artefacts. The cost of admission is around 10 AED ($2.72) per person.

- **Sharjah Arts Museum**: Art lovers will admire the extensive collection of contemporary and traditional art on display here. The cost of admission is approximately 5 AED ($1.36) per person.

- **Al Qasba**: Take a leisurely boat trip down the gorgeous Al Qasba Canal, which is studded with restaurants and cafes.

  A day trip to Sharjah from Abu Dhabi is estimated to cost around 30-50 AED ($8 - $14) per person.

Please keep in mind that the estimated expenses may change based on personal preferences, transportation options, and additional activities or attractions visited.

Consider arranging tours or using group transportation services to save money. Additionally, when organising your day trips from Abu Dhabi, always check for any new entrance fees and ticket costs.

Chapter 10

Sustainable Travel in Abu Dhabi

Green Initiatives in Abu Dhabi

Abu Dhabi is dedicated to encouraging environmentally friendly practices and protecting its natural resources. To promote sustainable travel and conserve the environment, the city has developed many green projects, including:

- **Masdar City**: Masdar City is one of the world's most sustainable metropolitan developments, focusing on renewable energy and eco-friendly technologies.

Visitors are welcome to visit this future eco-city that serves as an example of sustainable living.

- **Sustainable Transportation**: To reduce carbon emissions, Abu Dhabi supports the use of public transportation, cycling, and walking.

The city's increasing public transport infrastructure includes buses and proposals for a future metro, making it easier for residents and tourists to get around in an environmentally friendly manner.

- **Wildlife Conservation**: Abu Dhabi is committed to wildlife conservation.

Several nature reserves, such as Sir Bani Yas Island, are located in the city, where endangered animals are preserved and visitors can watch them in their natural settings.

- **Green construction practices**: Many new Abu Dhabi developments follow green construction standards, using energy-efficient designs and materials.

The renowned Sheikh Zayed Grand Mosque, for example, incorporates environmental practices into its design.

- **Water Conservation**: As a desert metropolis, Abu Dhabi prioritises water conservation. Water-saving techniques are frequently used in hotels and establishments, and tourists are encouraged to utilise water properly during their stay.

Responsible Travel Tips for Conscious Travelers

As an environmentally conscious traveller in Abu Dhabi, you can help to promote sustainable travel practises and reduce your environmental effect by doing the following:

1. **Respect Local Customs**: Embrace the local culture and customs, dress modestly, and avoid potentially insulting behaviours.

2. **Choose Environmentally Friendly Accommodations**: Choose hotels or resorts that have implemented environmentally friendly practices such as energy-saving systems, recycling programmes, and water conservation measures.

3. **Support Local Businesses**: Help the local economy by shopping at local stores, restaurants, and artists. Choose locally manufactured and sustainable souvenirs over things made from endangered species or unsustainable resources.

4. **Reduce your consumption of single-use plastic** by carrying a reusable water bottle and shopping

bag. Filtered water replenishment stations are available at many Abu Dhabi establishments.

5. **Conserve Energy**: Conserve energy by turning off lights, air conditioning, and other electronic devices when not in use. During your visit, be mindful of your energy consumption.

6. **Respect Wildlife**: When participating in outdoor activities such as wildlife tours, follow the organisers' recommendations and respect the natural habitats of animals and plants.

7. **Visit Wildlife Reserves and Eco-Friendly Attractions to Support Wildlife Conservation**: Consider visiting wildlife reserves and

eco-friendly attractions that support wildlife conservation efforts. Your admission prices and contributions frequently assist to fund conservation activities.

8. **Use Public Transportation**: To lessen your carbon footprint while exploring the city, use Abu Dhabi's public transportation system, such as buses and the coming metro.

By implementing these environmentally aware travel recommendations into your vacation to Abu Dhabi, you can help maintain the city's natural beauty, support sustainable efforts, and contribute to a greener and more ecologically conscious travel experience.

Be a conscious traveller who has a good impact on the places you visit.

Chapter 11

Abu Dhabi Travel FAQ

Frequently Asked Questions (FAQ)
about Travel to Abu Dhabi:

Q1: When is the best time of year to visit Abu Dhabi?

A1: The winter months, from November to March, are ideal for visiting Abu Dhabi because the weather is warm and appropriate for outdoor activities.

Avoid the sweltering heat of the summer months, which last from June to September, when temperatures can reach 40°C (104°F).

Q2: *What currency is used in Abu Dhabi?*

A2: The United Arab Emirates Dirham (AED) is the currency in Abu Dhabi.

Q3: *Will I require a visa to visit Abu Dhabi?*

A3: Visa requirements differ according to nationality.

Many countries' citizens are eligible for visa-free entrance or visa-on-arrival for a limited time. Before you travel, make sure you verify the visa requirements.

Q4: How common is English in Abu Dhabi?

A4: English is commonly spoken and understood in Abu Dhabi, particularly in tourist districts, hotels, and large establishments.

Q5: What are Abu Dhabi's key attractions?

A5: Attractions in Abu Dhabi include the Sheikh Zayed Grand Mosque, the Louvre Abu Dhabi, Ferrari World, Yas Waterworld, and Corniche Beach. Visitors can expect to see cultural landmarks, modern architecture, and thrilling activities.

Q6: How do I navigate Abu Dhabi?

A6: Taxis, public buses, and auto rentals are among the mobility alternatives available in Abu Dhabi. The Abu Dhabi Metro will give an extra way of transit in the future.

Q7: Is Abu Dhabi a secure place to visit?

A7: Yes, Abu Dhabi is regarded as a safe city for visitors. It boasts a low crime rate and a strong security system.

However, as with any other destination, conventional care and attention to your valuables are required.

Q8: Can I consume alcoholic beverages in Abu Dhabi?

A8: Alcohol is available for purchase in licenced hotels, restaurants, and pubs. Public intoxication and drinking in non-designated areas, on the other hand, are strictly prohibited.

Q9: Is there a dress code in Abu Dhabi?

A9: Abu Dhabi is a conservative city, therefore visitors should dress modestly when visiting religious sites and government buildings. Swimwear is permitted on beaches and in pools, but not in public places.

Q10: Should I be mindful of any cultural norms?

A10: Yes, local customs and traditions must be respected. Public shows of affection are discouraged, and guests should refrain from eating, drinking, or smoking in public throughout the holy month of Ramadan.

Local Expert Travel Advice:

1. **Stay Hydrated**: The UAE's environment can be hot, so staying hydrated by drinking enough water is critical, especially during outdoor activities.

2. **Plan for Ramadan**: If you're travelling during Ramadan, keep in mind that

many restaurants and cafes will be closed throughout the day. It's a fantastic opportunity to partake in traditional Iftar feasts after sunset.

3. **Check Dress Codes**: To minimise inconvenience, dress modestly and appropriately before visiting religious institutions or government facilities.

4. **Respect Local Customs**: Be respectful and kind to the locals, and embrace the local culture and customs.

5. **Taste Emirati Cuisine**: Don't pass up the opportunity to enjoy authentic Emirati meals like Arabic coffee, shawarma, and delectable desserts like kunafa and luqaimat.

6. **Use Sun Protection**: Because the sun can be harsh, use sunscreen, sunglasses, and a hat to shield yourself from its rays.

7. **Keep Ramadan Rules in Mind**: During Ramadan, avoid eating, drinking, or smoking in public during daylight hours. Some restaurants and cafes may be closed during the day but reopen after the sun goes down.

8. **Remove Your Shoes**: You may be obliged to remove your shoes before entering someone's home or specific areas.

9. When visiting traditional souks, bargaining is usual practice, so feel free to bargain for a better price.

10. **Learn a Few Basic Arabic Phrases**: Knowing a few basic Arabic phrases can be beneficial and appreciated by locals.

You can have a fulfilling and courteous experience while experiencing the attractions of Abu Dhabi if you follow this travel advice and learn local customs.

Chapter 12

Abu Dhabi Travel Resources

Essential Websites and Apps

1. Visit Abu Dhabi (*website: www.visitabudhabi.ae*): Abu Dhabi's official tourism website offers a wealth of information about sights, events, hotels, and practical travel advice.

2. Abu Dhabi Culture (*website: www.abudhabiculture.ae*):This website is a wonderful resource for staying up to date on Abu Dhabi's cultural offerings for cultural events, exhibitions, and performances.

3. Google Maps (App): A must-have app for navigating Abu Dhabi and finding sites of interest. It offers real-time traffic reports as well as directions to major sites.

4. Uber/Careem (Apps): Ride-hailing apps such as Uber and Careem provide convenient and dependable transportation inside Abu Dhabi.

5. Talabat (App): For people looking to order meals, Talabat is a popular app for food delivery from numerous Abu Dhabi eateries.

6. Abu Dhabi Events (http://www.abudhabievents.ae)

This website is dedicated to listing upcoming Abu Dhabi events, concerts, festivals, and cultural gatherings.

7. **The Entertainer (App)**: If you're looking for discounts and bargains on food, events, and attractions in Abu Dhabi, The Entertainer app is a wonderful place to start.

8. **Weather Abu Dhabi (App)**: This app provides reliable and timely weather information in Abu Dhabi, allowing you to stay up to date on weather prediction.

9. **Hala Abu Dhabi (App)**: With this app, you can simply order an Abu Dhabi cab and track your ride in real-time.

10. **Google Translate (App)**: For visitors who do not speak Arabic, Google Translate is a useful app for translating text and speech between languages.

Printed in Great Britain
by Amazon

27972810R00056